STUDY GUIDE

Sounder

William H. Armstrong

WITH CONNECTIONS

HOLT, RINEHART AND WINSTON
Harcourt Brace & Company

Austin • New York • Orlando • Atlanta • San Francisco • Boston • Dallas • Toronto • London

Staff Credits

Associate Director: Mescal Evler

Manager of Editorial Operations: Robert R. Hoyt

Managing Editor: Bill Wahlgren

Executive Editor: Emily Shenk

Component Editor: Stephen Wesson

Editorial Staff: *Assistant Managing Editor,* Mandy Beard; *Copyediting Supervisor,* Michael Neibergall; *Senior Copyeditor,* Mary Malone; *Copyeditors,* Joel Bourgeois, Jon Hall, Jeffrey T. Holt, Jane M. Kominek, Susan Sandoval; *Editorial Coordinators,* Marie H. Price, Jill Chertudi, Mark Holland, Marcus Johnson, Tracy DeMont; *Support Staff,* Pat Stover, Matthew Villalobos; *Word Processors,* Ruth Hooker, Margaret Sanchez, Kelly Keeley

Permissions: Carrie Jones, Catherine Paré

Design: *Art Director, Book & Media Design,* Joe Melomo

Image Services: *Art Buyer, Supervisor,* Elaine Tate

Prepress Production: Beth Prevelige, Sergio Durante

Manufacturing Coordinator: Michael Roche

Development Coordinator: Diane B. Engel

TABLE *of* CONTENTS

FOR THE TEACHER

Using This Study Guide 2

Tips for Classroom Management 3

Strategies for Inclusion 4

Assessment Options 5

About the Writer 6

About the Novel 7

Key Elements: Plot / Theme / Characters / Setting / Point of View / Imagery / Allusion 8–12

Resources Overview ....inside front cover	**Answer Key** 45–54

FOR THE STUDENT

Before You Read: Activities 13

Chapters I–II: Making Meanings / Choices 14–15

Chapters III–V: Making Meanings / Choices 16–17

Chapters VI–VIII: Making Meanings / Choices 18–19

Novel Projects: Cross-Curricular Connections / Multimedia and Internet Connections 20–21

Exploring the Connections: Making Meanings 22–24

    Lob's Girl, by Joan Aiken 22

    The Smartest Human I Ever Met: My Brother's Dog Shep, by Victor Villaseñor 22

    Moco Limping, by Daniel Nava Monreal 22

    Spirits of the Railway, by Paul Yee 23

    Learning to Read and Write, from The Narrative of the Life of Frederick Douglass, by Frederick Douglass 23

    Lonesome Valley (Anonymous) 24

    I Believe I Can Fly, by R. Kelly 24

    David and Goliath, from I Samuel 17, adapted by Diane B. Engel........................ 24

Novel Notes: Issues 1–6 25–30

Reading Skills and Strategies Worksheets: Novel Organizer / Visualizing Scenes /

    Charting Causes and Effects / Using a Time Line 31–35

Literary Elements Worksheets: Imagery / Allusion 36–37

Glossary 38

Vocabulary Worksheet 39

Test 41–44

Using This Study Guide

This Study Guide is intended to

- *help students become active and engaged readers*
- *deepen students' enjoyment and understanding of literature*
- *provide you with multiple options for guiding students through the novel and the Connections and for evaluating students' progress*

Most of the pages in this Study Guide are reproducible so that you can, if you choose, give students the opportunity to work independently.

Key Elements

- plot summary and analysis
- major themes
- character summaries
- notes on setting, point of view, and other literary elements

Making Meanings

- First Thoughts
- Shaping Interpretations
- Connecting with the Text
- Extending the Text
- Challenging the Text

A **Reading Check** focuses on review and comprehension.

The Worksheets

- **Reading Skills and Strategies Worksheets** focus on reading and critical-thinking strategies and skills.
- **Literary Elements Worksheets** guide students in considering and analyzing literary elements (discussed in **Key Elements**) important to understanding the novel.
- **Vocabulary Worksheets** provide practice with Vocabulary Words. Activities target synonyms, affixes, roots, context clues, and other vocabulary elements.

For the Teacher

About the Writer Biographical highlights supplement the author biography that appears in the HRW Library edition of this novel. Sidebars list works by and about the writer as resources for teaching and for students' research.

About the Novel A critical history summarizes responses to the novel, including excerpts from reviews. Sidebars suggest audiovisual and multimedia resources.

Key Elements Significant literary elements of the novel are introduced. These elements recur in the questions, activities, worksheets, and assessment tools.

For the Student: reproducible masters

Before You Read: Activities *(preparation for beginning the novel)*
Motivating activities lead students to explore ideas and topics they will encounter in the novel.

Making Meanings *(for each section of the novel)* Questions move students from immediate personal response to high-level critical thinking.

Choices: Building Your Portfolio *(for each section of the novel)* The activities suggested here involve students in exploring different aspects of the novel on their own or collaboratively. The results may be included in a portfolio, developed further, or used as springboards for larger projects.

Novel Projects *(culminating activities)* Cross-Curricular, Multimedia, and Internet projects relate to the novel as a whole. Project ideas can be adapted for individual, pair, or group presentations.

Exploring the Connections *(a set of Making Meanings questions for each of the Connections readings)* Questions encourage students to relate the readings to the themes and topics of the novel.

Novel Notes *(multiple issues)* These one-page news sheets provide high-interest background information relating to historical, cultural, literary, and other elements of the novel. They are intended for distribution *after* students have begun the novel section the issue supplements.

Reading Skills and Strategies Worksheets *(one for each section of the novel, plus a Novel Organizer)*

Literary Elements Worksheets *(end of novel)*

Vocabulary Worksheets *(during or after reading)*

Glossary, with Vocabulary Words *(to use throughout the novel)* This list of words from the novel serves as a mini-dictionary that students may refer to as they read. **Highlighted Vocabulary Words** support vocabulary acquisition.

Test *(end of novel)* A mix of objective and short-answer questions covering the whole novel provides a traditional form of assessment. Essay questions consist of five optional writing prompts.

Tips for Classroom Management

Preparing Students for Reading

Set aside a time each week for talking about books. On the right are some ideas for introducing a novel and motivating students to pick it up and begin reading.

Reading and Responding

Book groups Although most students will read independently, discussions with classmates can enrich their reading enormously. This Study Guide suggests appropriate points to stop and talk about the story so far. At these stopping points, the **Making Meanings** questions can be used as discussion starters. Ask groups to keep a simple log of their discussions.

Full-class discussions Engage students by beginning the discussion with a question that encourages a personal response (see **First Thoughts** in **Making Meanings**). As students respond to the questions involving interpretation, invite them to support their inferences and conclusions with evidence from the text. Encourage a noncritical environment. Show your own enthusiasm for the novel—it's infectious!

Reader's logs Logs, journals, and notebooks offer an open and nonthreatening yet systematic mode for students to respond in writing to the novel. Making entries as they read can help students learn more about themselves as readers, monitor their own progress, and write more easily and fluently. Keeping logs can also enhance participation in small-group and class discussions of the novel. Consider dialogue journals in which two readers—a student and you, a classmate, or a family member—exchange thoughts about their reading. **Reader's Log** suggestions appear in each issue of **Novel Notes**.

Cooperative learning Small groups may meet both to discuss the novel and to plan and work on projects related to the novel (see ideas in **Choices** and in **Novel Projects**). Encourage full participation by making sure that each group member has a defined role and that the roles rotate so that the same student is not always the leader or the recorder, for example.

Projects While students' projects can extend into other content areas, they should always contribute to enriching and extending students' understanding of the novel itself. If students know when they begin the novel that presenting a project will be a part of their evaluation, they can begin early to brainstorm, discuss, and try out ideas. Project ideas can come from **Novel Notes,** from the **Choices** activities, from the **Novel Projects** ideas, and, of course, from the students themselves. Projects can be developed and presented by individuals, pairs, or groups.

Reflecting

When students finish the novel, they should not be left with a test as the culminating experience. Project presentations can be a kind of celebration, as can a concluding discussion. On the right are some ideas for a reflective discussion. They can be used in a whole-class environment, or small groups can choose certain questions to answer and share their conclusions (or their disagreements) with the class.

Ideas for Introducing the Novel

- Give a brief book talk to arouse students' curiosity and interest (see **About the Novel** for ideas).

- Play or show a segment of an audio, film, or video version of the book or an interview with the writer.

- Present high-interest biographical information about the writer (see **About the Writer** in this Study Guide and the biographical sketch at the end of the HRW Library edition of this novel).

- Read aloud a passage from the novel that arouses your own interest, and elicit predictions, inferences, and speculations from students.

- Lead a focused class discussion or suggest activities that (1) draw on students' prior knowledge or (2) lead them to generate their own ideas about a significant topic or theme they will encounter in the novel (see **Before You Read).**

Reader's Log Starters

- When I began reading this book, I thought…
- My favorite part, so far, is…
- I predict that…
- I like the way the writer…
- I'd like to ask the writer…
- If I had written this book, I would have…
- This [character, incident, idea] reminds me of…
- This book made me think about…
- This book made me realize…

Questions for Reflection

- What was your favorite part of the book (and why)?

- If you could be one of the characters, who would it be (and why)?

- Would you or wouldn't you recommend this book to a friend (and why)?

- What is the most important thing about this book?

- Would you change the ending? If not, what makes it work? If yes, what changes would you make?

- If you could have a conversation with the writer, what would you say or ask?

Strategies for Inclusion

Each set of activities has been developed to meet special student interests, abilities, and learning styles. Because the questions and activities in this Study Guide are directed to the students, there are no labels to indicate the types of learners they target. However, in each Before You Read, Choices, and Novel Projects page, you will find activities to meet the needs of

- *less proficient readers*
- *students acquiring English*
- *advanced students*

The activities and projects have been prepared to accommodate these different learning styles:
- *auditory/musical*
- *interpersonal*
- *intrapersonal*
- *kinesthetic*
- *logical/mathematical*
- *verbal/linguistic*
- *visual/spatial*

Using the Study Guide Questions and Activities

Encourage students to adapt the suggestions given in the Study Guide to fit their own learning styles and interests. It is important to remember that students are full of surprises, and a question or activity that is challenging to an advanced student can also be handled successfully by students who are less proficient readers. The high interest level, flexibility, and variety of these questions and activities make them appropriate for a range of students.

Students should be encouraged to vary the types of activities they choose so that the same student is not regularly selecting writing or researching activities over those involving speaking, art, and performing, and vice versa. Individual and group work should also alternate, so that students have the opportunity to work on their own and as part of collaborative learning groups.

Working in Pairs and Groups

When students with varying abilities, cultural backgrounds, and learning styles work together, they can arrive at a deeper understanding of both the novel and one another.

Reading pairs can stop and check each other's responses to the novel at frequent intervals.

Students from different cultural groups can interview one another about how certain situations, character interactions, character motivations, and so on would be viewed in their home cultures.

Visualizing and Performing

Students who have difficulty with writing or with presenting their ideas orally can demonstrate their understanding of the novel in a variety of ways:

- making cluster diagrams or sketching their ideas

- creating tableaux showing where characters are in relation to one another during a scene, their poses or stances, and their facial expressions

- creating thought balloons with drawings or phrases that show what a character is thinking at a given moment

- drawing their own thoughts in thought balloons above a sketched self-portrait

- listing or drawing images that come to mind as they read or hear a certain section or passage of the novel

- making a comic-book version of the novel (with or without words)

- coming to class as a character in the novel

Assessment Options

Perhaps the most important goal of assessment is to inform instruction. As you monitor the degree to which your students understand and engage with the novel, you will naturally modify your instructional plan. The frequency and balance of class and small-group discussion, the time allowed for activities, and the extent to which direct teaching of reading skills and strategies, literary elements, or vocabulary is appropriate can all be planned on the basis of your ongoing assessment of your students' needs.

Several forms of assessment are particularly appropriate for work with the novel:

Observing and note taking Anecdotal records that reflect both the degree and the quality of students' participation in class and small-group discussions and activities will help you target areas in which coaching or intervention is appropriate. Because communication skills are such an integral part of working with the novel in a classroom setting, it is appropriate to evaluate the process of making meaning in this social context.

Involving yourself with dialogue journals and letters You may want to exchange notes with students instead of, or in addition to, encouraging them to keep reader's logs. A powerful advantage of this strategy is that at the same time you have the opportunity to evaluate students' responses, you can make a significant difference in the quality of the response. When students are aware that their comments are valued (and addressed to a real audience, an audience that writes back), they often wake up to the significance of what they are reading and begin to make stronger connections between the text and their own lives.

Agreeing on criteria for evaluation If evaluation is to be fair, it must be predictable. As students propose and plan an activity or project, collaborate with them to set up the criteria by which their work will be evaluated, and be consistent in applying only those criteria.

Encouraging self-evaluation and goal setting When students are partners with you in creating criteria for evaluation, they can apply those criteria to their own work. You might ask them to rate themselves on a simple scale of 1, 2, or 3 for each of the criteria and to arrive at an overall score. Students can then set goals based on self-evaluation.

Peer evaluation Students can participate in evaluating one another's demonstrations and presentations, basing their evaluations upon a previously established set of standards. Modeling a peer-evaluation session will help students learn this method, and a chart or checklist can guide peer discussion. Encourage students to be objective, sensitive, courteous, and constructive in their comments.

Keeping portfolios If you are in an environment where portfolios contain only carefully chosen samples of students' writing, you may want to introduce a second, "working," portfolio and negotiate grades with students after examining all or selected items from these portfolios.

Opportunities for Assessment

The suggestions in this Study Guide provide multiple opportunities for assessment across a range of skills:

- demonstrating reading comprehension
- keeping reader's logs
- listening and speaking
- working in groups—both discussion and activity-oriented
- planning, developing, and presenting a final project
- acquiring vocabulary
- taking tests

Questions for Self-evaluation and Goal Setting

- What are the three most important things I learned in my work with this novel?
- How will I follow up with these so that I remember them?
- What was the most difficult part of working with this novel?
- How did I deal with the difficulty, and what would I do differently?
- What two goals will I work toward in my [reading/writing/group work, etc.]?
- What steps will I take to achieve those goals?

Items for a "Working" Portfolio

- reading records
- drafts of written work and project plans
- audio- and videotapes of presentations
- notes on discussions
- reminders of cooperative projects, such as planning and discussion notes
- artwork
- objects and mementos connected with themes and topics in the novel
- other evidence of engagement with the book

For help with establishing and maintaining portfolio assessment, examine the **Portfolio Management System** *in* **Elements of Literature.**

About the Writer

More on Armstrong

MacCann, Donnarae, and Gloria Woodard, eds. *The Black American in Books for Children: Readings in Racism.* Metuchen, N.J.: Scarecrow Press, 1972.

Townsend, John Rowe. *Written for Children: An Outline of English-Language Children's Literature.* New York: Lippincott, 1974. Includes a discussion of the literary and cultural merits of *Sounder.*

Also by Armstrong

Barefoot in the Grass: The Story of Grandma Moses. New York: Doubleday, 1970. This biography gives rich details about the life and times of the painter Grandma Moses.

The Education of Abraham Lincoln. New York: Coward, 1974. This biography dramatizes the early life of Abraham Lincoln.

The MacLeod Place. New York: Coward, 1972. In this novel, two farmers struggle to save their farm when they learn that the government plans to build a highway through it.

The Mills of God. New York: Doubleday, 1973. This novel is set in the Appalachian Mountains during the Great Depression. It vividly depicts the era as it tells the story of a boy named Aaron and his dog.

Sour Land. New York: HarperCollins, 1971. In this novel, Moses Waters, an elderly teacher, earns the trust of his students but experiences prejudice and violence.

A biography of William H. Armstrong appears in Sounder, *HRW Library edition. You may wish to share the following additional biographical information with your students.*

Even though William H. Armstrong grew up in the historic Shenandoah Valley of Virginia, and set many of his books and stories in the southeastern United States, he has lived most of his life as a writer and teacher in New England. When he was in his early twenties, Armstrong moved to Kent, Connecticut, to teach history at a private school, and ended up staying for more than fifty years.

When Armstrong began writing books in his forties, he started with study guides and history books. In his first book, *Study Is Hard Work,* Armstrong explains the importance of keeping a study schedule—a practice that he rigorously applies in his own work. Armstrong sets aside three hours each morning for writing, from 4:00 A.M. until 7:00 A.M., because, he explains, he likes to have a big job done each day before sitting down to breakfast. He refuses to write with a computer or even a typewriter, and instead produces his work using a pencil on a tablet of lined paper. In 1969, Armstrong used these simple tools to write his first novel, *Sounder,* which went on to win the Newbery Medal and find readers around the world.

Although Armstrong has written more than a dozen books, he still doesn't think of himself primarily as a writer. When asked what he does, Armstrong says that he's a teacher, and that he'd much rather work with stone and wood than write.

About the Novel

CRITICAL COMMENT

Sounder won immediate praise and honors upon its publication in 1969. George Wood, children's editor for *The New York Times Book Review,* called it the best novel of 1969. Alice Walker described it in *The New York Times Book Review* as "painful, stunning poetry." June Meyer Jordan, also in *The New York Times Book Review,* commented that, in *Sounder,* "We are urged into participation, a moral questioning and a moral wonder. When we stop reading, we want to hear the living voice, the distinctively human sound of this anonymous, black family."

The novel has been described as having epic qualities. Zena Sutherland, writing in the *Bulletin of the Center for Children's Books,* says that *Sounder* is "written with quiet strength and taut with tragedy. . . . Grim and honest, the book has a moving, elegiac quality that is reminiscent of the stark inevitability of Greek tragedy."

Sounder has been criticized for its portrayal of African Americans. For example, in *The Black American in Books for Children: Readings in Racism,* Albert V. Schwartz complains that the book stereotypes the black experience in America. He criticizes *Sounder* because "Black language, a vital and historic means of communication for the creation of a story of Black people, is totally absent. . . ." He also comments that the author's failure to give any member of the sharecropping family a name denies "human individualization to the Black person." Evelyn Geller complains of its "moral limitations—its nostalgic evocation of endurance with all hostility . . . repressed."

Other critics, however, disagree. Diane G. Stavn, in the *School Library Journal,* writes, "The human characters' namelessness lends them universality as oppressed people, while [Armstrong's] authentic, detailed descriptions of their particular appearance, home, food, and hard-to-casually-brutal environment assure their individuality. . . . An utterly effective depiction of the repressive environment makes readers understand that the characters lack behavioral options: they are neither ineffectual nor cowardly, but heroic and noble; seeming passivity is really a quiet, stoical dignity."

Awards and Honors

Newbery Medal

Lewis Carroll Shelf Award

Mark Twain Award

For Viewing

Sounder. Paramount Home Video, 1972. Award-winning adaptation of the novel featuring Cicely Tyson and Paul Winfield. (A sequel—***Sounder, Part 2***—came out in 1976.)

Key Elements

Make a Connection

Have students discuss the family's difficult circumstances as the story begins—their isolation, their straitened finances, and their lack of access to formal education. Discuss what resources might be available to the family in an emergency, and how they might go about solving a life-or-death problem.

Plot

Chapters I–II As the novel opens, the boy is standing with his father on the porch of their cabin. The boy wants to talk about Sounder, the great coon dog who helps the father hunt to support the family, but the father doesn't want to talk about the dog. It is winter, hunting is bad, and the family has little to eat. That evening, the father leaves the house without Sounder, and in the morning, sausage and ham are cooking on the stove. A few days later, a sheriff and two deputies arrive and arrest the father for stealing the meat. As they haul the father away in a wagon, Sounder breaks free and runs to help his master. A deputy shoots Sounder, wounding him terribly. Sounder crawls under the house, so far back that the boy cannot find him, however far he looks.

Chapters III–V The next morning, while the mother goes to return the remaining sausage and ham, the boy searches again for Sounder but does not find his body. When the mother returns, she suggests that Sounder may not be dead—that he might have gone off alone to heal. Weeks pass, though, and the dog does not return. When Christmas arrives, the mother makes a cake and the boy takes it to his father in jail. The jailer smashes the cake, looking for tools or weapons. He treats the boy roughly, and the father tells the boy not to come again. That night, Sounder finally returns to the house, permanently maimed. Some days later, the family learns that the father has been sentenced to hard labor, but they do not know where he will be—or for how long.

Chapters VI–VIII Years pass as the boy works to help his family, going on long journeys in search of his father whenever he can. One day, while the boy is on one of his long searches, he meets a schoolteacher, who invites him to his home for water. When the teacher learns about the boy's desire to learn, he invites the boy to live with him and attend his school. The boy agrees to go to school every autumn, but returns home each summer to help his family. Then, one August day, Sounder sees a stranger hobbling up the road and lifts his mighty voice for the first time in years. It is the boy's father, finally returning home after six years of imprisonment. The father has been severely injured in a mining accident, however, and a few months after his return, he dies quietly in the woods while on a hunting trip with Sounder. Sounder himself dies a few months after his master, but the memory of the great coon hound remains with the boy into his adulthood.

Key Elements *(continued)*

Plot Elements The boy faces **external conflicts** as he deals with the absence of his father. He undertakes several difficult journeys in which he has to travel through strange territory and endure abuse from strangers—first, his journey into the jail to speak to his father, and then his several years of searching across the state. In addition, the boy faces **internal conflicts** as he yearns for formal education but does not know how he might attain it.

Theme

Students will see the following **themes,** or main ideas, developed in detail in *Sounder.*

The Power of Love Although the ordeals faced by the family in *Sounder* can seem terribly cruel, most of the key events in the book are brought about by the powerful emotional bonds between the characters. It is the father's love for his family that compels him to find food for them, which in turn brings about his long incarceration. Similarly, the boy's love for his father sends him on lonely, dangerous journeys across the state—but these travels also help him begin his formal education. The love of the family in *Sounder* is a powerful force, but it does not shelter the family from harm or from the injustices of the society they live in.

The Power of Injustice For hundreds of years, African Americans have had to face injustices due to racial prejudice. In *Sounder,* these injustices are played out under the harsh light of a rigidly segregated society. The father bears perhaps the cruelest injustice when he is given a long and ultimately fatal sentence for a minor crime committed to help feed his family. Throughout the book, however, the sharecropper family must contend with unjust treatment in most aspects of their daily lives, from the humiliations dealt out by law officers to the life of hard labor and little hope that the parents must face because of their lack of formal education.

Make a Connection

Guide a discussion of injustice, and invite students to give examples. Ask them whether injustice is always the result of a specific action, or whether it can also be the result of inaction. Discuss ways in which injustices can be overcome.

Connecting with Elements of Literature

You can use *Sounder* to extend students' examination of the themes and topics presented in *Elements of Literature.*

- *Introductory Course:* "Justice for All," Collection Five
- *First Course:* "Living in the Heart," Collection Five
- *Second Course:* "We Shall Overcome: American Struggles and Dreams," Collection Eight

Key Elements (continued)

Make a Connection

Point out that the author does not give names to most of the characters. Discuss how your students think this might affect how well they can get to know the characters.

Characters

Students will meet the following **characters** in *Sounder.*

The boy is the central character of the novel. Armstrong provides little description of the boy, and never mentions his specific age, although he seems to be about eleven when the novel begins and about seventeen when it ends. At first, the boy is timid though inquisitive, but by the end of the book he has gained confidence and established his independence.

The father appears only briefly in the novel, but his absence through most of the book is very powerfully felt. He seems quiet and guarded at the beginning of the book, and his few words are very important to the boy.

The mother is hard-working and self-sacrificing; she holds the family together through terrible circumstances with her calm presence. She is keenly aware of the dangers the family faces and quietly focuses on what she must do to guarantee their survival.

The teacher is a kind, gentle, and understanding man who quickly grasps the boy's hunger for learning.

Sounder is a great coon dog with an undying love for the family. Part Georgia redbone hound and part bulldog, he is a powerful creature whose name reflects his loud, clear, melodious voice. Sounder's willingness to suffer for his family and his loyalty over long, difficult years illustrate one of the book's major **themes:** the power of love. Sounder is the only character in the novel who is given a name.

Make a Connection

Remind students that Armstrong grew up in the southeastern United States, the region in which this story takes place. Call on volunteers to share impressions that they have about this part of the country. As students read the novel, encourage them to look for ways in which the novel is similar to or different from other depictions of the region that they might have read or seen.

Setting

The novel takes place somewhere in the southeastern United States, probably in Georgia, about a hundred years ago, although Armstrong never specifies a time or place. The major and minor conflicts of the novel grow directly from this **setting.** African Americans experienced severe restrictions and unfair treatment, both by law and by common practice, in the rural southeast at the turn of the century. The boy has to navigate this treacherous landscape of hardship and abuse as he tries to find his father, and as he tries to secure a better future for himself.

Point of View

Armstrong tells the story of *Sounder* from a **limited third-person point of view.** The reader has access to the thoughts and feelings of the boy as he negotiates the novel's major and minor **conflicts,** and knows his impressions of his parents and the other characters. Armstrong does not, however, describe the thoughts and feelings of the book's other characters—indeed, the boy's siblings are barely even mentioned, let alone described. The reader instead comes to see the problems and events of the book through the boy's eyes alone.

Imagery

The story of *Sounder* is told using very simple language, but the novel is rich in vivid **description,** often created by the effective use of **imagery,** or language that appeals to the senses. Although most imagery is visual—creating pictures in the mind—it can also appeal to the senses of hearing, touch, taste, and smell. Consider this example from *Sounder:*

> Suddenly the voice of the great coon hound broke the sultry August deadness. The dog dashed along the road, leaving three-pointed clouds of red dust to settle back to earth behind him. The mighty voice rolled out upon the valley, each flutelike bark echoing from slope to slope.

This example includes imagery that uses the senses of touch ("sultry August deadness"), sight ("dog dashed along the road, leaving three-pointed clouds of red dust to settle back to earth behind him"), and hearing ("mighty voice rolled out upon the valley, each flutelike bark echoing").

Make a Connection

Discuss the ways in which **point of view** can change how a story is told. As students read *Sounder,* discuss how the story might be told from the boy's point of view or from the mother's.

Make a Connection

Invite students to look around the classroom and describe what they see. Encourage them to enhance their **descriptions** by including **imagery**—especially images that appeal to senses other than sight.

A *Literary Elements Worksheet* that focuses on imagery appears on page 36 of this Study Guide.

A *Literary Elements Worksheet* that focuses on allusion appears on page 37 of this Study Guide.

Allusion

An **allusion** is an indirect reference to someone or something from literature, history, religion, mythology, or another field. Allusions enrich the reading experience by providing, in just a few words, an additional layer of meaning and emotional content. In Chapter VII of *Sounder,* for example, a prison guard hurls a piece of iron at the boy, mashing his fingers on the fence. As the boy walks away, the guard throws a second piece of iron. The boy imagines picking it up and throwing it at the guard's head:

> And the stone that David slung struck Goliath on his fore-
> head; the stone sank into his forehead, and he fell on his
> face on the ground, the boy thought.

This allusion to the biblical story of David and Goliath adds the heroic flavor of that story to the boy's encounter. The boy deals with his feelings of anger and powerlessness by thinking of David, who, as a boy, conquered a giant who threatened the people of Israel.

Before You Read

Activities

MAKING PERSONAL CONNECTIONS

Pondering Pets

Have you ever heard the saying that a dog is a person's best friend? (As you read *Sounder*, you will have the chance to see this saying at work.) How do you feel about pets? Use your experience or imagination to write two lists: "The Ten Best Things About Having a Pet" and "The Ten Hardest Things About Having a Pet." If you wish, work with classmates to create a bulletin-board display with your lists. As a class, talk about the rewards that pets can bring—and the care and training that pets need.

BUILDING ON PRIOR KNOWLEDGE

With Liberty and Justice for All?

In many ways, *Sounder* is a story about racial injustice. What do you know about race relations during the time in which *Sounder* takes place? Do you think that all Americans were treated equally and had equal opportunities? With some of your classmates, discuss some of the difficulties an African American family might have faced a hundred years ago. Then, as you read *Sounder*, see whether your thoughts are confirmed or change.

SHARING OPINIONS

Down on the Farm

The main characters of *Sounder* live in an isolated cabin in a rural area, and depend on farming and hunting for their living. What would life in those circumstances be like? Discuss this question with a group of classmates. Try to get every-one in the group to comment on how that way of life might be similar to or different from his or her own life in the areas of education, food, work, social life, and entertainment.

DISCUSSING

One Person's Story

Read Armstrong's note at the start of *Sounder* about the man who taught him to read. Then, talk about these questions as a class:

- Can you picture this older man in your mind? What do you think he looked like?
- Why do you think he held "a lasting, magnificent intoxication" in Armstrong's mind?
- Why might he have been the only African American ever to visit Armstrong's church?
- Why does Armstrong think that the story about Sounder is important? Do you think it really happened?

Novel Notes

Use **Novel Notes, Issue 1**

- to find out more about some of the topics and themes in *Sounder*
- to get ideas for writing activities and other projects that will take you deeper into the book

Making Meanings

First Thoughts

1. What do you think of the father so far? Do you agree with his actions?

Shaping Interpretations

2. As the novel begins, the father doesn't want to talk about the dog. As he listens to the wind, what might be weighing upon his mind?

3. While cooking on the morning after the father returns, the mother hums to herself. How do you know that trouble may be on the way?

READING CHECK

a. Why is the family dog named Sounder?

b. What does the father bring home for his family?

c. Who are the men that come to the cabin on the third evening? What do they want?

d. What does Sounder do when the father is taken away? What happens to Sounder?

e. What does the boy think has become of Sounder?

4. The **atmosphere** or **mood** of a piece of writing is its overall "feeling." How does the atmosphere of this story change during the first two chapters?

5. At the end of Chapter II, the mother regrets asking her son why he has filled Sounder's food dish. What is the mother thinking?

Connecting with the Text

6. The father says nothing during his arrest. When shots are fired, the father doesn't even look. If these things happened to you, would you behave so quietly? Why or why not?

Extending the Text

7. The sheriff responds harshly to the father's crime of stealing food for his family. Could this kind of arrest take place in today's society? Explain why or why not.

Challenging the Text

8. Some critics have said that the mother shows no feelings or love toward her children. Based on what you know about her so far, do you agree? Why or why not?

Choices: Building Your Portfolio

COOPERATIVE LEARNING

Tackling Topics

First, brainstorm with your class to produce a list of topics that are important in this section of the novel. You might start things off with traits of the main **characters, symbolism,** or **plot** predictions. Then, with a partner, discuss one topic and make a list of the three things your class should know about this topic. After five minutes, share your ideas with the class.

ART

Let Me Illustrate . . .

What do you think is the most memorable **scene** in this first section of *Sounder?* Make a drawing, sculpture, or painting to illustrate the scene. Be prepared to explain your artwork to the class, or work with some classmates to create a "gallery walk" of your finished pieces.

SPEAKING AND LISTENING

The Sound of *Sounder*

Although *Sounder* is prose, it has a musical, rhythmic style that often sounds like poetry. Discover this poetry for yourself by doing a reading with a partner. First, choose a passage that is about a page long. Then, read the selection out loud, with you and your partner reading every other sentence. Read slowly, using emphasis, pauses, and careful pronunciation to bring the writing to life. If there are any words that you aren't familiar with, make a list of them and discuss them with your partner to decide what they might mean. Afterward, discuss why you think Armstrong chose to use this style in his novel, and what you think it adds to the book.

CREATIVE WRITING

In Her Eyes

The mother says little in this section of the novel. Still, Armstrong gives us brief glimpses into what she might be thinking. Choose one **scene** from this section of the book, and write it from the mother's **point of view,** being careful to include what she is feeling and thinking as the scene develops. Consider presenting your rewrite as a **dramatic monologue,** in which you read "in character," as if you were the mother.

Consider This . . .

But there was no price that could be put on Sounder's voice. . . . it was not an ordinary bark. It filled up the night and made music as though the branches of all the trees were being pulled across silver strings.

What makes Sounder's voice so special? Do you think the boy and his family are aware of his special talents?

Writing Follow-up: Causes and Effects ▪

What do you think would cause such a dog to be valued so highly by the father and son? What might be the effects of Sounder's disappearance?

Novel Notes

Use **Novel Notes, Issue 2**

- to find out more about some of the topics and themes in Chapters I–II
- to get ideas for writing activities and other projects related to *Sounder*

Making Meanings

READING CHECK

With two classmates, take turns retelling the events of this section. While your classmates narrate, listen carefully to be sure they include all important details.

First Thoughts

1. Respond to these chapters by completing these sentences.

   • If I were the mother, knowing that I had four children to support, I would feel . . .

   • If I were the father, knowing that I could no longer help my family, I would feel . . .

Shaping Interpretations

2. The mother returns the uneaten sausage and ham. What **motivation,** or guiding reason, might push her to do this?

3. Why do you think the mother urges her son to stop looking for Sounder?

4. One of the **themes** of this novel is "The Power of Love." How could the father's telling the boy not to come again to visit him in jail be a loving action?

5. Think about where the **plot** leaves you at the end of Chapter V. How do you think Armstrong wants you to feel at this point—optimistic or pessimistic? Explain your answer.

Connecting with the Text

6. No one in the family really knows what will happen to them from one day to the next. How do you think this uncertainty makes the family feel? How does uncertainty make you feel?

Extending the Text

7. The family has no way of learning what is happening to the father or where he is being sent. Could such a total break in communication happen today? Why or why not?

Challenging the Text

8. By the end of Chapter V, the father is gone, and Sounder is no longer able to hunt. In your opinion, should the writer have explained how the family survives without these important sources of income? Why or why not?

Choices: Building Your Portfolio

READER'S THEATER

A Dramatic Moment

With a few classmates, select a dramatic **scene** from Chapters III–V of *Sounder* and prepare it as a Reader's Theater presentation. Look for a scene that has important **action,** such as the boy's search under the house for Sounder, or sharp **conflict,** such as when the boy attempts to take a cake to his father in jail. Practice your presentation and perform it for your class.

BUILDING VOCABULARY

Terms Lost in Time

What are *overalls* and a *tin-topped table?* Do you know what a *fencerow* is? What about *straw tick* or a *visiting preacher?* Make a list of these and any other terms from *Sounder* that are unfamiliar to you. Then, meet with a group of classmates. Share the words on your lists and work together to find the meaning of each one. Work together to create a bulletin-board display of the terms and their meanings, with illustrations.

SMALL-GROUP WORK

Still to Come

By the end of Chapter V, Sounder has returned and the boy's father has been sentenced to hard labor somewhere in the state. A few questions have been answered, but many more remain. What do you think will happen in the final chapters of the novel? Meet with a group of classmates and discuss the possible developments. After you have heard your classmates' ideas, jot down your predictions. Then, continue reading *Sounder* to find out which predictions come true.

CREATIVE WRITING

Showdown!

Confronting a bully—as the boy does when he meets the "large red-faced man" at the jail—is a story idea that is almost guaranteed to hold a reader's interest. Either on your own or with a partner, write a short story, with a **setting** that is different from the one in *Sounder,* about someone who is forced into a showdown with a bully. Your story can be very short—maybe only a few paragraphs in length—but it should have a clear beginning, middle, and end. Share your story with the class, either by reading it or by acting it out.

Consider This . . .

There on the cabin porch, on three legs, stood the living skeleton of what had been a mighty coon hound.

Sounder has returned, but in what condition? If you were the boy, how would you feel at this moment as you looked at your dog?

Writing Follow-up: Reflecting ■

What things in your life might make you feel the same mixture of emotions that the boy experiences?

Novel Notes

Use **Novel Notes, Issue 3**

- to find out more about some of the topics and themes in Chapters III–V
- to get ideas for writing activities and other projects related to *Sounder*

Making Meanings

First Thoughts

1. Describe your thoughts about the ending of *Sounder.*

Shaping Interpretations

2. The teacher tells the boy that it is hard to reset a plant that has wilted, but that a plant that shows new growth will be all right. What do you think the plant **symbolizes,** or represents?

3. Throughout the novel, the mother keeps singing and humming bits of the spiritual "Lonesome Valley." How is this song important to the story?

4. In these chapters, how does the boy show his persistence? How is he rewarded?

5. How are Sounder and the boy's father alike?

READING CHECK

a. Describe what happens to the boy as he stands outside a prison camp, watching the convicts whitewashing stones.

b. What does the boy see a man throw into a trash barrel? Why is the boy disappointed when he recovers it?

c. What big news does the boy share with his mother after he returns from his journey? What is his mother's response?

d. Why does Sounder become excited when he sees the figure hobbling down the road?

e. What does the boy do for Sounder before leaving for school near the novel's end?

6. At the end of the novel, the boy remembers a special comment from his book: "Only the unwise think that what has changed is dead." Restate this comment in your own words.

Connecting with the Text

7. The boy and his mother, although saddened by the deaths of the father and Sounder, remain calm and peaceful. Why do you think they are able to accept the deaths of their loved ones so quietly?

Extending the Text

8. How can reading and literature contribute to your understanding of events in your daily life?

Challenging the Text

9. Some readers have criticized *Sounder* because the main characters seem to accept the injustices done to them calmly and without anger. What do you think, and why?

Choices: Building Your Portfolio

COOPERATIVE LEARNING

Theme Hunt

Hunting is important to Sounder and his family, so do some hunting of your own. Work with a few classmates to choose one of the novel's major **themes:** "The Power of Love" or "The Power of Injustice." Then, take turns, in round-robin fashion, and give examples from this section of the story to illustrate that theme. When you have named all the examples you can, try a "hunt" on the other theme.

EXTENDED READING

A Moment with Montaigne

Obtain a copy of Montaigne's *Essays* and find some of the essays mentioned or alluded to in *Sounder.* Read some passages from these essays, as well as other essays from the book. Share your impressions of the essays with your classmates and explain why you think Armstrong chose this book for the boy to find.

ROLE-PLAYING

Interview with the Boy

With your classmates, brainstorm a list of specific questions you would like to ask the boy. Some questions might refer to specific details from this section of *Sounder* or to the novel as a whole. Other questions might extend the story. Then, meet with a small group and imagine that the boy is visiting your classroom. Take turns playing the role of the boy while the rest of the group interviews him. Afterward, discuss how this activity helps you understand him and his story better.

CREATIVE WRITING

The Boy Grown Up

Re-read the Author's Note at the beginning of *Sounder.* Then, imagine how the solitary, eloquent man described there might have told this story. On your own or with a partner, rewrite one **scene** from this final section of the novel as you think that adult would relate it.

Consider This . . .

"In Bible stories everybody's always goin' on a long journey. . . . And in Bible-story journeys, ain't no journey hopeless. Everybody finds what they suppose to find."

The boy uses this argument to persuade his mother to let him search for his father. Would you be persuaded?

Writing Follow-up: Persuading

Suppose that the boy's mother does not find this argument persuasive. What arguments would you use to help the boy talk his mother into letting him search?

Novel Notes

Use **Novel Notes, Issue 4**

- to find out more about some of the topics and themes in Chapters VI–VIII
- to get ideas for writing activities and other projects related to *Sounder*

Cross-Curricular Connections

MUSIC

Sorrowful Songs

At several points in *Sounder,* the mother sings or hums the spiritual "Lonesome Valley." A spiritual is a type of folk song that traces its history back through the time of slavery. With a few classmates, locate and then perform or play recordings of spirituals and folk songs from the southeastern United States. As you share the songs, you might also give some information about their history. Afterward, discuss how the thoughts expressed in these songs relate to the thinking of the people you have met in *Sounder.*

SOCIAL STUDIES

Racial Equality: How Have Times Changed?

For the sharecroppers in *Sounder,* the idea of racial equality in the United States must have seemed like a dream that might never come true. Has that dream come true? With a few classmates, do some investigation. Consider equality of education, job opportunities, fair housing, and other topics that may be suggested during your research. As a group, choose the information that you want to share. Then, hold a panel discussion to present your findings and conclusions to the class. Use graphs and charts to help make your presentation clear, and allow time for questions.

ART

Mural, Mural, on the Wall

With a group of classmates, create a mural based on *Sounder.* Be sure to include **settings** and **scenes** from the novel, as well as the boy, his family, Sounder, and some of the other **characters.** Some members of your group might do sketches; others might research details or check the accuracy of the drawings; and others might work on coloring or painting the sketched mural. When you finish, display your mural for the class to discuss and appreciate.

LANGUAGE ARTS

A Eulogy for Sounder

Think about the boy's reaction when he hears that Sounder has died: "The boy was glad." Why does he feel this way, especially about a dog that he considers "a human animal"? Imagine that the boy has decided to write and deliver a eulogy for Sounder. What might the boy say about the dog? What did Sounder mean to him and his family? Deliver your finished eulogy to the class and ask for comments.

MUSIC

Capturing Sounder's Sound

Re-read the description of Sounder's voice in Chapters I and VIII. How do you think it might sound as a melody that humans would appreciate? If you play a musical instrument, create a simple tune that makes you think of Sounder's voice and play your composition for the class. If you do not play a musical instrument, find a piece of simple recorded music, such as a composition featuring trumpets or other horns, and play it for the class. Discuss the ways in which your version of the sound of Sounder is different from what your classmates imagine it to be.

Multimedia and Internet Connections

NOTE: Check with your teacher about school policies on accessing Internet sites.

RADIO: DRAMA

Sounder Theater

When William H. Armstrong was a young man, radio plays were as popular a form of entertainment as television programs are today. Radio drama has been called "Theater of the Mind," because each listener creates mental images of the characters and settings in the story. Work together with other students to write and perform a radio adaptation of one or more scenes from *Sounder.* Use Armstrong's dialogue, include a narrator, and add music or sound effects where you think they will help. Make an audiotape of your performance and play it for the class, or perform it for them live.

FILM: VIEWING AND REVIEWING

Screening Room

Not only was *Sounder* adapted for the movies in 1972, but a sequel (written by the co-writer of the screenplay for *Sounder,* not by Armstrong himself) was made four years later. Watch a video of the first film and see how it compares to the book. For example, how do the characters and settings in the movie differ from what you imagined as you were reading the book? What details were left out, and what details were added? If you were the filmmaker, what might you have done differently? Present your opinions to the class. If your class has access to video equipment, show parts of the movie to illustrate your points.

INTERNET: POSTING COMMENTS

Everyone's a Critic

See what other readers think of *Sounder* by reading critical reviews of the novel on Web sites. Write an essay in response to one of the reviews, either agreeing or disagreeing with the writer. Be sure to offer specific details and examples to support your opinion, and be courteous and respectful of the other writer's opinion.

INTERNET: RESEARCH

Coon Hounds in Cyberspace

Like just about everyone else, coon hounds are on the Internet. See what you can find out about them by searching on the World Wide Web and share your findings with your class in a presentation. Use these questions to guide your research:

- Which dog breeds are used as coon hounds?
- Which coon hound breeds are recognized by the kennel clubs?
- What are the characteristics of good coon hounds?
- How are coon hounds judged in competition?
- What are the best ways to take care of these dogs?

Exploring the Connections

Making Meanings

Lob's Girl

Novel Notes
See *Issue 5*

1. What do you think of Lob? Why?

2. Why do you think that the **title** of this story is "Lob's Girl" rather than "Sandy's Dog"?

3. In her **description** of the fishing village, Aiken makes it a point to mention the "narrow, steep, twisting hill-road" and the sign that warns drivers and cyclists. What do these details **foreshadow**—that is, how are they clues about what will happen later?

4. How is Lob like Sounder? How is he different?

5. Have you ever had a pet that showed special devotion to you or to someone in your family? If so, describe the situation. If not, describe a situation from a movie, TV program, or other story that demonstrates the devotion of an animal for a human.

> **READING CHECK**
>
> What are two important **scenes** from the story? Draw a quick sketch of these two scenes, adding as much detail as you think is necessary.

The Smartest Human I Ever Met: My Brother's Dog Shep / Moco Limping

Novel Notes
See *Issue 5*

1. How would you feel about Moco or Shep if either of these dogs were your own? Explain.

2. In "Moco Limping," what does the speaker mean when he says, "My vain heart weeps/knowing he/is mine"?

3. How is Sounder similar to the dog that the speaker of this poem would like to have? How is Sounder similar to Moco?

4. In "The Smartest Human I Ever Met: My Brother's Dog Shep," why does the **narrator** refuse to believe Rosa's explanation for Shep's barking? Give at least two reasons.

5. Compare Shep's relationship with Joseph to Sounder's relationship with the father in *Sounder*.

> **READING CHECK**
>
> **a.** How is the dog Moco different from the dog that the speaker would like to have?
>
> **b.** According to Rosa, why is Shep racing around and howling?
>
> **c.** What explanation does Rosa give for Shep's disappearance?

Making Meanings

Spirits of the Railway

Novel Notes
See *Issue 6*

1. What **scene** from the story stands out the most in your mind? Why?

2. What words or phrases would you use to describe the **character** of the younger Chu?

3. How is the older Chu's life like that of the father in *Sounder?*

4. "The Power of Injustice" is an important **theme** in *Sounder.* How is that theme also illustrated in this story?

5. Do you think the older Chu and the father in *Sounder* might view the events that shorten their lives in a similar way?

> **READING CHECK**
>
> **a.** Why does the older Chu leave China?
>
> **b.** How does he die?
>
> **c.** What must the younger Chu do so that his father's ghost can rest?

Learning to Read and Write

Novel Notes
See *Issue 6*

1. Just for a moment, put yourself in the shoes of Frederick Douglass. How would you feel about being denied an education?

2. How did learning to read make Douglass more discontented?

3. Douglass says that the woman who began to teach him to read changed as a result of slavery. How do you think slavery brought about this change in her?

4. Based on how Douglass describes his life in this selection, was education good for him? Why or why not?

5. Douglass was enslaved in his youth; the boy in *Sounder* is free. How are their lives similar?

6. Although Douglass very much wants to learn to read, his owners won't allow it. Have you ever wanted to do something very badly—only to be forbidden? How did you feel?

> **READING CHECK**
>
> With two of your classmates, list the methods that Frederick Douglass used to learn how to read and write. Compare your list with lists from other groups of classmates.

Exploring the Connections

Making Meanings
Lonesome Valley / I Believe I Can Fly

Novel Notes
See **Issue 6**

1. These songs present different views of life as a quest. Which song appeals to you more? If you completed the For Your Reader's Log activity in **Novel Notes, Issue 6,** check your notes for a comparison of different quests.

> **READING CHECK**
>
> **a.** What is the **main idea** of "Lonesome Valley"?
>
> **b.** What is the **main idea** of "I Believe I Can Fly"?

2. Because they are passed along orally, many folk songs have more than one set of lyrics, or words. Compare the lyrics to "Lonesome Valley" in this version with the lyrics sung by the mother in *Sounder.* Why do you think Armstrong chose the lyrics that he did?

3. Do you think that the boy in *Sounder* would agree or disagree with the message in "I Believe I Can Fly"? Explain why or why not.

4. Imagine that your school is planning to adopt one of these two songs as its theme song. Think about the goals and purposes of your school. Which song would be better? Why?

David and Goliath

1. Respond to this Bible story by completing these sentences.

    • If I were standing before Goliath, I would think . . .

    • If I were in the Philistine army and saw Goliath killed, I would think . . .

> **READING CHECK**
>
> **a.** What bargain does Goliath offer the army of Israel?
>
> **b.** Why is David not afraid to fight Goliath?
>
> **c.** What happens when David fights Goliath?

2. What is the effect of the detailed description of Goliath's helmet, spear, coat of mail, and other armor?

3. King Saul knows what will happen if David loses to Goliath. In your opinion, why does he allow this young boy to represent his entire army in this winner-take-all fight?

4. When the prison guard in *Sounder* throws a piece of iron and injures the boy's hand, the boy remembers the story of David and Goliath. What might this story mean to him at that moment?

5. The story of David and Goliath teaches that it is possible for people to overcome great odds. How useful is this advice in everyday situations?

Novel Notes

Issue 1

Introducing SOUNDER

Trapped on the Farm

In the decades after the Civil War, many poor rural families had to work as *sharecroppers*—that is, as farm laborers who didn't own the land they farmed. Under the sharecropping system, a sharecropper planted and grew crops on someone else's land. When the harvest was sold, the landowner got a share of what the land produced—often as much as one half.

Because they were paid only after the harvest, sharecroppers usually had to borrow money to live on for most of the year. After the landowner's share of the crop money was taken out, there often wouldn't be enough money left for the sharecropper to pay the previous year's debt, and the debt would grow from year to year. This cycle of poverty and dependence kept some sharecropping families tied to one farm for generations, until the sharecropping system was finally eliminated in the middle of the twentieth century.

Missing ABCs

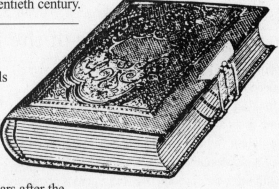

During the years of slavery, the majority of African Americans seldom received any education whatsoever—education was too difficult to obtain for most free African Americans, and in most slave states it was illegal to teach slaves to read. Following the Civil War, African Americans began to attend school in greater numbers, but formal education was still very difficult to obtain. In much of the country, schooling was segregated by race, and schools that taught African Americans were often scarce and poorly funded. Despite these obstacles, in the years after the Civil War, increasing numbers of African Americans learned to read and write, and in the decades that followed, African Americans fought to gain even greater educational opportunities.

The Word PLACE

Sounder takes place on a farm in the southeastern United States about one hundred years ago. These are some of the terms used to describe the objects the characters use and the place where they live.

bottomland: the low, flat land along a river, often very rich farmland

burlap sack: a bag made of a very coarse, heavy cloth

coal oil: kerosene, an oil made from petroleum and used as fuel in lanterns and lamps

fencerow: the fence that borders a field or pasture, including trees and shrubs growing along it

ticking: a heavy, sturdy cloth, often striped, used to make covers for pillows and mattresses and to patch clothing

SOUNDER Chapters I–II

A Breed Apart

The great coon hound Sounder is part Georgia redbone hound and part bulldog—a great combination for a raccoon hunting dog.

Bulldogs are squat, muscular dogs, usually with huge heads and pushed-in noses. Bulldogs were given their name centuries ago in England, when they were bred to fight bulls. This brutal sport has long since been outlawed, but bulldogs are still known for their powerful jaws and great determination.

Redbone hounds are North American hunting dogs that were specifically bred to hunt raccoons. Redbones generally weigh between 45 and 60 pounds, and usually have the distinctive red coloring that gives the breed its name. Redbone hounds are known for their speed and intelligence, as well as for their loud, melodious voices. Redbone hounds have tremendous determination, and have been used to hunt opossums, mountain lions, and even bears.

FOR YOUR READER'S LOG

What must life have been like for a poor share-cropper family like the one in *Sounder?* What would the people have done for fun? What made them laugh? As you read these chapters, jot notes about their daily lives.

The Melody of the Hunt

The call of the coon hound has for many years been the sound of a successful hunt. Raccoon hunting takes place after dark, when raccoons are most active, and visibility is sometimes a problem. When hunting dogs pick up the scent of a raccoon, they immediately begin the chase and track the raccoon over hills, across ponds and streams, and through swamps. A chase can last for hours, or even all night, and the dogs bay every so often so the hunters will know where the hunt is headed. When the raccoon is finally "treed"— that is, when it climbs a tree to escape the dogs— the coon hounds set up a steady barking, and the hunters hurry to catch up with them. On a long hunt, the dogs are often far ahead of the hunters, and so the strength of a dog's voice is especially important. Dogs that have voices as strong and as clear as Sounder's, however, are prized for the beauty of their call as well as for their hunting ability.

The Masked Bandit

Raccoons—or coons, as they are sometimes called—are small, stocky animals with long, thick fur. They have long tails with ringlike stripes, and are well known for the black band of fur over their faces that makes them look like masked bandits. Raccoons have been hunted for hundreds of years for sport, for food, for their fur and to prevent them from damaging crops or livestock. However, their very high intelligence, along with their strong swimming and climbing abilities, makes raccoons very challenging opponents.

Novel Notes

Issue 3

SOUNDER Chapters III–V

What's Cooking?

Sharecroppers rarely had the chance to eat as well as the landowners they worked for—much of the time, they had to get by on leftovers and foods the landowners didn't want. Over time, they found ways to stretch these odds and ends into delicious meals, many of which are still traditional Southern dishes.

chitlins: Also called *chitterlings* and *Kentucky oysters,* these are the small intestines of pigs. Usually they are prepared by first boiling and then frying.

corn mush: A mainstay of Southern cooking, corn mush is made by combining cornmeal with water or milk and simmering the mix until it looks like pudding.

dumplings: Dumplings are small pieces of dough that are simmered in broth and served with a main dish.

milk gravy: Usually gravy is made by combining and cooking milk, flour, and grease from meat, which adds flavoring. When times are tough, the gravy might be made without adding grease.

sow belly: Also known as *salt pork,* this is a fatty meat taken from the back, side, or belly of a hog.

❧ Take Two Acorns and Call Me in the Morning ☙

Dogs have been known to go off to heal themselves by lying in oak leaves. This might sound like an unusual treatment to people who buy their medicine at a pharmacy, but it is one of the many plant-based cures that were once common in the United States. Oak leaves, oak bark, and even acorns are still valued by herbal healers for their ability to stop bleeding.

In Other Words

A *symbol* is a person, place, thing, or event that has a meaning in itself and that also stands for something else. For example, a book might symbolize a person's hunger for education or the power of the imagination.

Symbols aren't always obvious, and can take many different forms. A burlap sack, a long journey, and even the sound of someone's voice can all be used to carry unexpected—and sometimes enlightening—meanings.

Novel Notes

Issue 4

SOUNDER Chapters VI–VIII

Workin' on a Chain Gang

The *chain gang* was a common form of punishment in the nineteenth and early twentieth century. Prisoners on a chain gang were chained to each other, usually by their legs, and put to work on hard, dangerous tasks. Because they were prisoners, convicts on chain gangs were treated much worse than ordinary workers would ever be—they were overworked, poorly fed, and sometimes beaten badly. Some states earned money by leasing the chain gangs to private businesses, such as mines and sawmills, or used the convicts' labor for state projects, such as road construction. Reforms in the early twentieth century dramatically reduced the use of chain gangs but did not completely eliminate them.

> **FOR YOUR READER'S LOG**
>
> If you could talk with the boy about his years searching for his father, what questions would you like to ask him? As you read, jot questions in you Reader's Log.

 ## Steal Away

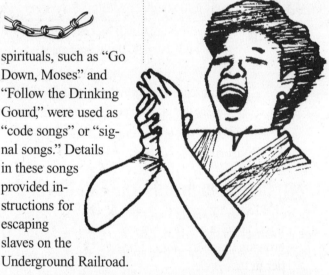

During the years of slavery, a new form of music arose that was unique to the United States—the African American spiritual. Spirituals were religious songs based on subjects from Bible stories. They were sung using a mixture of African and North American musical styles. At first, spirituals were mostly sung in the churches, houses, and fields of African American slaves, but after the Civil War, spirituals became popular across the country.

Spirituals were not used exclusively in religious worship. Some spirituals, such as "Go Down, Moses" and "Follow the Drinking Gourd," were used as "code songs" or "signal songs." Details in these songs provided instructions for escaping slaves on the Underground Railroad.

THE BOOK IN THE TRASH CAN

Michel de Montaigne (mee-SHEL duh mohn-TAYN) was a French lawyer and writer who lived in the late 1500s. Montaigne had a successful career as a lawyer, a diplomat, and a mayor, but never derived satisfaction from his political life. After his best friend, another young writer, died suddenly, Montaigne began to withdraw from public life, and eventually retreated to his country home and spent all his time reading and writing.

The result of these years alone was the *Essays,* a remarkable collection of Montaigne's writings on a wide variety of topics, ranging from friendship, education, and idleness to death, lying, and even cannibalism! In the *Essays,* Montaigne explores his thoughts in a series of short, informal compositions. These brief personal meditations have been read for over four hundred years. They gave their name to a form of writing you might have used yourself—the essay.

Novel Notes

SOUNDER Connections

* A M E R I C A N   W R I T E R S *
Joan Aiken

Joan Aiken, the writer of "Lob's Girl," is an American who grew up in England, surrounded by books and writers. When she was five, Aiken began writing poems and stories of her own, which she published while she was still in school. Later, she recalled that she was never paid for her poems, which taught her an important lesson: Poets don't make a lot of money. Nevertheless, Aiken continued her writing, concentrating instead on short stories and novels. Among her novels are *The Wolves of Willoughby Chase, Night Fall, The Whispering Mountain,* and *Midnight Is a Place.*

Connections

- **Lob's Girl**
- **The Smartest Human I Ever Met: My Brother's Dog Shep**
- **Moco Limping**

FOR YOUR READER'S LOG

Why are dogs such good companions? As you read these Connections, list the characteristics that make dogs so appealing to their human friends.

BOOK Bytes

Check out these stories about remarkable dogs:

- *The Call of the Wild,* by Jack London. The story of a powerful and loyal sled dog who leads teams of sled dogs over the wilds of Alaska.
- *Old Yeller,* by Fred Gipson. A novel about a boy and his dog growing up on the Texas frontier in the 1860s.

Going to the Dogs

- *Ramu and Chennai, Brothers of the Wild,* by Michael W. Fox. A novel about a young boy who learns about life in the jungle by raising a wild dog.
- "Snapshot of a Dog" and "The Dog That Bit People," by James Thurber. Hilarious short stories about the author's own dogs.
- *Stay! Keeper's Story,* by Lois Lowry. A dog tells this story about his experiences living with different humans.

ASK the Professor

Dear Dr. I. Knoweverything,
My uncle, who's hard of hearing, says he's about to get a "hearing dog." I know about dogs that help people with vision trouble, but are there really dogs that help people with hearing impairments?
—Dog Days in Durango

Dear Days,
You might be surprised by how many different kinds of assistance dogs there are. Most people know about guide dogs or pilot dogs, which help people with impaired vision get around by guiding them around obstacles. Hearing dogs, on the other hand, help their owners by serving as hearing assistants—if a doorbell rings or a pot is about to boil over, a hearing dog can let its owner know.

Another type of assistance dog, the service dog, can help people with mobility impairments live independently. A service dog might be trained to pull a wheelchair, pick up dropped items, open doors, carry groceries, and turn on lights for its owner.

Novel Notes

SOUNDER Connections

Incredible Journey

In "Spirits of the Railway," both the younger Chu and his father make long and difficult journeys in search of a better life. Their journeys are fictional, but not too different from those made by real people throughout history.

- **Immigration** Between the early 1800s and the 1930s, more than thirty million people immigrated to the United States from all parts of the world. They sought freedom, economic opportunity, and peace, but many had to endure the same hardships experienced by young Chu.

- **Trail of Tears** In 1838 and 1839, the U.S. Army forced more than fifteen thousand Cherokee people to travel a thousand miles from their homes in the southeastern U.S. to what is now Oklahoma. Thousands died of malnutrition, exposure, disease, and bad treatment on this journey, which became known as the Trail of Tears.

- **Underground Railroad** It wasn't a real railroad—it was a secret escape route for thousands of American slaves who sought freedom in the North. The runaways risked severe punishment if caught and faced enormous dangers in their journey to freedom.

- **Pacific Island Migration** Thirty-five hundred years ago, a group of people began settling the widely scattered islands of the Pacific Ocean. Although they didn't have compasses, the people somehow found their way in canoes across nearly two thousand miles of open ocean. Eventually they settled on every habitable island in the Pacific from Hawaii to New Zealand.

Connections

- **Spirits of the Railway**
- **Learning to Read and Write**
- **Lonesome Valley**
- **I Believe I Can Fly**

The Word PLACE

Any *Questions?*

A *quest* is a long journey in search of someone or something. The word comes from a Latin word that means "to ask," and is related to the word *question,* appropriately enough—if you want to find something, you're probably going to have to ask plenty of questions. Quests are very common in literature. A quest story might feature knights in search of treasure or knowledge or heroes in search of adventure. A quest can be a search for something much more serious, though, such as an education or a missing parent.

Reading Skills and Strategies Worksheet

Novel Organizer   *Sounder*

CHARACTER

Use the chart below to keep track of the characters in this book. Each time you come across a new character, write the character's name and the number of the page on which the character first appears. Then, jot down a brief description. Add information about the characters as you read. Put a star next to the name of each main character.

NAME OF CHARACTER	PAGE	DESCRIPTION

Reading Skills and Strategies Worksheet

Novel Organizer *(continued)*   *Sounder*

SETTING

Where and when does this story take place? ....

....

....

CONFLICT (Read at least one chapter before you answer.)

What is the biggest problem faced by the main character(s)? ....

....

....

How do you predict it will be resolved? ....

....

....

MAJOR EVENTS

- ....
- ....
- ....
- ....
- ....

OUTCOME

How is the main problem resolved? (How accurate was your prediction?) ....

....

....

Name _____ Date _____

Reading Skills and Strategies Worksheet

Sounder

Chapters I–II: Visualizing Scenes

Filmmakers use **storyboards**—drawings that illustrate key moments in a film—
to keep track of their stories. Suppose that you planned to film this first section
of *Sounder.*

**For each of the headings below, sketch the main scene you would
want to film. Give each scene in your storyboard a caption that
explains the action.**

The Boy Takes Pride in Sounder	A Delicious, Dangerous Smell
Caption:	*Caption:* ....

The Sheriff Arrives	Sounder to the Rescue
Caption:	*Caption:* ....

Reading Skills and Strategies Worksheet
Sounder

Chapters III–V: Charting Causes and Effects

A **cause** is what makes something happen. The **effect** is what happens. Recognizing causes and effects can help you understand events in a novel and what they mean. For example, the boy's father is arrested because he steals meat to feed his family. Because Sounder tries to help his master, the dog is shot.

Complete the following cause-and-effect chart. It will help you think about what happens in this part of *Sounder*—and why.

CAUSE	EFFECT
The mother knows that her son will crawl under the cabin, looking for Sounder.	
	The boy disobeys his mother and leaves the younger children alone at home.
	The boy's mother brings home vanilla flavoring.
Women are not allowed to visit the jail in town.	
	The man at the jail breaks the cake into pieces.
	The boy hears whining on the cabin porch.

Reading Skills and Strategies Worksheet

Sounder

Chapters VI–VIII: Using a Time Line

You can use a time line to track the key events in a story, play, or novel.

Complete the following time line to show eight of the most important events in this last part of *Sounder,* in the order in which they take place.

START OF CHAPTER VI

1. _____
2. _____
3. _____
4. _____
5. _____
6. _____
7. _____
8. _____

END OF CHAPTER VIII

Look back at all the events you listed. Which event do you think is most important? Write the event here and explain why you selected it.

....

....

....

....

....

....

....

Literary Elements Worksheet

Sounder

Imagery

Imagery is language that appeals to the senses. Writers use imagery to help readers experience the sights, sounds, smells, tastes, and textures of the worlds created by the writers.

Read each of the following passages from *Sounder*. Then, identify all the senses involved in each one: sight, hearing, smell, taste, or touch. Follow the instructions that follow each passage.

1. The woman watched each year for the walnuts to fall after the first hard frost. Each day she went with the children and gathered all that had fallen. The brownish-green husks, oozing their dark purple stain, were beaten off on a flat rock outside the cabin.

   Which senses are involved? ....
   Underline words or phrases that appeal to the sense of sight.

2. He stood close to the warm stovepipe, turning one cheek and then the other to its glowing warmth. . . . The warmth ran up his sleeves and down over his ribs inside his shirt and soaked inward through his whole body.

   Which senses are involved? ....
   Underline words or phrases that appeal to the sense of touch.

3. He hurt his knees and elbows on broken glass, rusty sardine cans, and broken pieces of crockery and dishes. The dry dust got in his mouth and tasted like lime and grease. Under the cabin it smelled stale and dead, like old carcasses and snakes.

   Which senses are involved? ....
   Underline words or phrases that appeal to the sense of taste.

4. He warmed himself and watched a patch of red glow the size of his hand at the bottom of the stove. . . . After a long quiet spell the rocker began to squeak, and it made the boy jump, but his mother didn't notice. She began to rock as she picked out walnut kernels.

   Which senses are involved? ....
   Underline words or phrases that appeal to the sense of hearing.

5. Choose one of your favorite images from the novel and write it below.
   Then, identify which senses are involved.

   ....

   ....

Literary Elements Worksheet

Sounder

Allusion

An **allusion** is an indirect reference to someone or something from literature, history, religion, mythology, or another field. Allusions can add deeper meaning to a story.

Explain these allusions to Bible stories that appear in *Sounder*. (The first one is done for you. Sometimes more than one meaning is possible.)

1. *Allusion:* The mother tells her children about a "mighty flood" the Lord sent to wash away the evil in the world.

This allusion suggests that the mother would like to see the evil, or hardships, gone from the lives of her family.

2. *Allusion:* The boy remembers a story about Shadrach, Meshach, and Abed-nego, who were "thrown right into the jail stove" but were rescued by the Lord.

This allusion suggests that ....

....

3. *Allusion:* The boy reminds his mother that in the Bible "everybody's always goin' on a long journey," and that they all find "what they suppose to find."

This allusion suggests that ....

....

4. *Allusion:* The mother tells the boy about Joseph the dreamer, who was a slave and a prisoner, but who eventually became "the Big Man in Egypt."

This allusion suggests that ....

....

5. *Allusion:* During his long search for his father, the boy remembers that King David heard the sound of the wind in the trees and knew that the Lord was fighting for his army.

This allusion suggests that ....

....

6. *Allusion:* When the prison guard hits the boy with a piece of metal, the boy remembers the story of David, who killed Goliath with a stone from a sling.

This allusion suggests that ....

....

Glossary

Sounder

- Words are listed by chapter in their order of appearance.
- The definition and part of speech are based on the way the word is used in the chapter. For other uses of the word, check a dictionary.
- **Vocabulary Words** are preceded by an asterisk (*) and appear in the **Vocabulary Worksheet.**

Chapter I

punctuated *v.:* interrupted

wavered *v.:* grew louder, softer, and then louder again; trembled

addled *adj.:* confused

Chapter II

ashen *adj.:* pale like ashes

mongrel *n.:* dog of mixed breed

entangled *adj.:* twisted together; tangled up

constrained *adj.:* in a forced, unnatural manner

plaintive *adj.:* expressing suffering; mournful

floundering *v.:* struggling clumsily

Chapter III

haunches *n.:* hindquarters of an animal

pallet *n.:* small bed or sleeping pad

rivulets *n.:* small streams

smart *v.:* hurt with a sharp, stinging pain

Chapter IV

poultice *n.:* soft, wet medicinal mass that is placed on a wound or sore

mange *n.:* skin disease of animals that causes itching

Chapter V

quarry *n.:* place where rock is dug out of the earth

famished *adj.:* very hungry

fret *v.:* worry

Chapter VII

fetch *v.:* go get something and bring it back

tote *v.:* carry

compulsion *n.:* forceful urge to do something

fruitless *adj.:* unsuccessful

gyrations *n.:* circular motions

malicious *adj.:* hateful; spiteful

animosity *n.:* strong, even hostile, resentment

cistern *n.:* large underground tank for storing water

commotion *n.:* noisy, confused activity

stoop *n.:* small entry porch with steps

sanctuary *n.:* safe, protected place

orneriness *n.:* consistently irritable attitude

mellow *adj.:* soft, full, pure; not severe

conjured *adj.:* under a magic spell

Chapter VIII

parched *v.:* dried up from heat

indistinct *adj.:* dim; not clearly visible

sultry *adj.:* very hot and damp

askew *adj.:* crooked; leaning to one side

Name _____ Date _____

Vocabulary Worksheet

Sounder

A. In the space provided, write the word from the box that best completes each sentence. (You will not use every word.)

commotion	sanctuary	parched	sultry	haunches	fruitless
cistern	punctuated	mange	famished	tote	mongrel

1. A loud howl _____ the silence of the dark countryside.

2. The _____ that lived by the lonely cabin howled at the moon.

3. The dog sat back on its _____ and howled long and loudly.

4. The poor animal had _____ and soon stopped barking to scratch itself vigorously.

5. There was no breeze on that _____ summer evening.

6. The cabin, which lacked air conditioning, was no _____ from the fierce heat.

7. The boy filled a bucket with water from the _____.

8. He would _____ the bucket to the pen and give the dog water.

9. Watering the garden would be _____, for the plants were already dead.

10. The sun had _____ the fields of corn, so there would be no harvest.

B. *Synonyms* are words that are the same (or nearly the same) in meaning. Choose the correct synonym for each word in dark type. Write the letter of that synonym in the space provided.

_____ **11. fetch: (a)** give **(b)** get **(c)** lose **(d)** hurt

_____ **12. indistinct: (a)** sharp **(b)** bright **(c)** dim **(d)** clear

_____ **13. askew: (a)** crooked **(b)** straight **(c)** broken **(d)** lost

_____ **14. entangled: (a)** angry **(b)** trapped **(c)** blocked **(d)** separated

_____ **15. constrained: (a)** unnatural **(b)** forgetful **(c)** carefree **(d)** typical

_____ **16. stoop: (a)** house **(b)** jail **(c)** door **(d)** porch

_____ **17. fret: (a)** worry **(b)** laugh **(c)** get **(d)** mourn

_____ **18. plaintive: (a)** happy **(b)** clear **(c)** sorrowful **(d)** helpful

_____ **19. wavered: (a)** decided **(b)** splashed **(c)** argued **(d)** trembled

_____ **20. pallet: (a)** bed **(b)** porch **(c)** sack **(d)** pillow

Notes

TEST   PART I: OBJECTIVE QUESTIONS

In the space provided, mark each true statement *T* and each false statement *F*. (20 points)

_____ **1.** The boy lives in a sharecropper cabin with his family and a dog named Sounder.

_____ **2.** The father steals money so that he can buy food for his family.

_____ **3.** The sheriff regrets having to arrest the father.

_____ **4.** Sounder disappears after the father is taken away.

_____ **5.** The mother goes to see her husband while he is in jail.

_____ **6.** The father is sentenced to serve a term of imprisonment at hard labor.

_____ **7.** After years of searching, the boy eventually finds his father at a road camp.

_____ **8.** The boy finds a book by a writer named Montaigne.

_____ **9.** Sounder barks because he recognizes the father returning from prison.

_____ **10.** The father is disappointed that the boy has left home to go to school.

Complete each statement by writing the letter of the best answer in the space provided. *(10 points)*

11. When the novel opens, the boy isn't going to school because _____.

    a. his father doesn't make him go   **c.** the school is too far away
    b. there is no school for him to attend   **d.** he is too young

12. Sounder stops barking after _____.

    a. the boy leaves home   **c.** the mother returns the meat
    b. it becomes too windy to hunt   **d.** the father is arrested

13. The boy's hand is hurt when _____.

    a. a prison guard throws a   **c.** a jailer slams a door on it
        piece of iron at him   **d.** he tries to protect his father
    b. he scratches it on a board

14. The teacher _____.

    a. tells the boy where his father is   **c.** explains that Sounder has gone
    b. invites the boy to stay with   off to heal himself
        him and attend school   **d.** gives the boy a book by Montaigne

15. Before returning to school at the end of the novel, the boy _____.

    a. gives his mother a book   **c.** digs a grave for Sounder
    b. tells his father goodbye   **d.** speaks at Sounder's funeral

TEST PART II: SHORT-ANSWER QUESTIONS

Answer each question, using the lines provided. (40 points)

16. Why is the dog named Sounder?

....

....

....

17. Why can't the father feed his family by hunting raccoons and possums anymore?

....

....

....

18. How does the father's clothing reveal that he stole the meat?

....

....

....

19. How does Sounder become injured?

....

....

....

20. What does the mother do with the meat after the father is arrested?

....

....

....

TEST PART II: SHORT-ANSWER QUESTIONS *(continued)*

21. What does the father tell the boy about visiting him at the jail anymore?

....

....

....

22. What is the boy carrying when he meets the teacher?

....

....

....

23. What impresses the boy about the teacher's home?

....

....

....

24. How does Sounder behave when he sees the father returning?

....

....

....

25. How does the father become injured while he is away?

....

....

....

TEST PART III: ESSAY QUESTIONS

Choose *two* of the following topics. Use your own paper to write two or three paragraphs about each topic you choose. *(30 points)*

a. Describe the time and place in which *Sounder* takes place. Then, describe the two aspects of the novel's setting that you believe are most important to the story.

b. Do you think that this story is mainly optimistic or pessimistic? Give reasons and examples from the text to support your answer.

c. Of all the **characters** in the novel, only the dog Sounder has a name. Why do you think the writer did not name the other characters? How might the novel be different if the characters were named?

d. Religion is an important part of the lives of the characters in *Sounder*. Give three examples of the role religion plays in the novel, including specific details from the text.

e. A **theme** is a main idea in a work of literature. Many themes reveal a writer's thoughts about life and relationships. In *Sounder*, Armstrong deals with subjects such as love, injustice, and the pursuit of goals. What do you think is the central theme of *Sounder?* Support your opinion with details from the novel.

Use this space to make notes.

Answer Key

Answer Key

Chapters I–II: Making Meanings

> **READING CHECK**
>
> **a.** He has a deep, mellow, flutelike voice that echoes across the valley.
>
> **b.** He brings home a ham.
>
> **c.** The sheriff and two deputies come to arrest the father for stealing the ham.
>
> **d.** He runs to chase the wagon and is shot.
>
> **e.** He thinks that Sounder is dead.

1. Some students may admire him as a responsible, hard-working person who does what he has to do to care for his family. Students may or may not agree with his decision to steal the food; encourage them to give reasons for their response.

2. Students may respond that the father is worrying about how he will feed his family, considering the ethics of stealing food, or weighing the risks of getting caught.

3. "His mother always hummed when she was worried," the boy thinks. As readers, we wonder what is worrying her now.

4. At the beginning of the novel, the atmosphere is one of comfort and safety. By the end of Chapter II, the atmosphere has become one of anxiety and foreboding.

5. Students may suggest that she is thinking that her son doesn't realize that Sounder is dead. She regrets her question because she realizes that the boy should keep believing that Sounder may yet be alive.

6. Answers will vary. Some students may say they would be more outspoken and much less passive. Some students, however, will find reasons to justify the father's stoic acceptance of his punishment, such as concern for his family.

7. Answers will vary. Some students may feel that such unjust punishments are still regularly meted out, but some may note advances in race relations since the time of *Sounder*. Encourage students to give reasons and examples, perhaps from current events, to support their responses.

8. Some students may say that the mother does show feeling and compassion. Although she doesn't talk much or express her feelings outwardly, she watches the boy carefully, and understands and responds to his feelings about the injury and possible death of Sounder.

Chapters III–V: Making Meanings

> **READING CHECK**
>
> Students should provide a detailed retelling of the plot of the section, including the boy's search for Sounder and the mother's response, the Christmas visit to the jail, Sounder's return, and news about the father's sentencing.

1. Answers for the mother may include *anxious, worried, uncertain, fearful, determined,* or *desperate.* Answers for the father may include *angry, helpless, depressed,* or *worried.*

2. She might be motivated by love for her husband, hoping that returning the food might ease his punishment. She may want to right a wrong. She also might be afraid to have something in the house that has caused such trouble, or afraid that she and her children will be punished further if they eat the stolen meat.

3. Students may see that the mother wants the boy to learn to accept loss rather than continue in a lost hope.

Answer Key (continued)   *Sounder*

4. Students may conclude that the father is trying to protect the boy from seeing him confined in a miserable environment—even if doing so deprives him of seeing the son he loves.

5. Some students will feel optimistic because Sounder is back, and because the family finally has word of what will happen to the father. The family also hopes that the father will get time off for good behavior and will send word of where he is being sent. Other students will feel pessimistic because the dog is permanently maimed and the father is being sent to hard labor. Moreover, the hopeful words about a short sentence and word of his whereabouts are not deeply felt by either the mother or the boy.

6. Students may believe that the family feels very insecure, worried, and fearful about the future. Students' other responses will be personal and need not be shared, but students are likely to regard uncertainty as an unpleasant feeling.

7. Some students will respond that such a lack of communication would be unlikely today, because communication technology, such as telephones and automobiles, is available to everyone. Some students may note, however, that hard times can still force families apart.

8. Answers will vary, but many students may feel that, considering the novel's preoccupation with the difficulties of survival, this aspect of the family needs to be explained more fully.

Chapters VI–VIII: Making Meanings

READING CHECK

a. A guard throws a piece of iron that mashes the boy's fingers. The boy imagines what his father would do if he were one of the convicts, but when nothing happens, the boy knows that his father is not there. He turns to walk away, and the guard throws another piece of iron. The boy imagines what would happen if he threw the iron back and hit the guard. Instead of throwing the metal, however, he walks away.

b. He sees the man throw a book in the barrel. He is disappointed because the words are hard and he doesn't understand the book.

c. He tells his mother that the teacher has asked him to come live with him and go to school. His mother considers it a sign and tells her son to go and learn.

d. Sounder realizes that the figure is his returning master.

e. The boy digs a grave for Sounder because he correctly suspects that the dog will not live much longer.

1. Some students may feel sad at the novel's end because the father and Sounder have died. Others will feel optimistic because the boy recognizes that his father and Sounder will live as long as he remembers them. Students may also point out that the boy has gained an education and built the foundation for a better life than his parents had.

2. The plant is a symbol for the boy, who has suffered a great deal and whose life has to be restarted. The boy still has a future, though, and is already starting over.

3. The song describes the journey of life, in which all people must live and endure suffering. It suggests the boy's journey in quest of his father and of knowledge, as well as his mother's lonely journey through life without her husband.

4. The boy persists in searching for his father until his mother urges him to go to school instead. He then persists at getting an education, and is rewarded by a greater understanding of the world.

5. Students may respond that both are strong, capable, and much admired at the beginning of the novel. Both suffer great injustices and injuries that deprive them of vigor and shorten their lives. Nevertheless, both endure and are eventually reunited with the people about whom they care the most.

6. Answers will vary but should reflect the idea that change is a part of life, and that both Sounder and the boy's father will live on in the boy's memories of them.

7. Answers will vary, but students may point to the family's religious faith as a source of comfort and acceptance. Other students may suggest that the family's long experience with deprivation has helped them to prepare themselves for cruel circumstances, however grievous and unjust.

8. Students should recognize that literature shows how other people have dealt with, or might deal with, personal events and that these insights may help them better understand events in their own lives.

9. Some students will point out that the boy sometimes dreams of revenge on his tormentors, and that these dreams demonstrate his anger. Furthermore, the characters' lack of open resistance may be a response to the realization that in their circumstances, resistance might achieve nothing and would likely endanger the family. Other students may comment that such restraint is unrealistic and that it is human nature to want to respond to injustice in some way, however difficult the circumstances.

Exploring the Connections

Lob's Girl: Making Meanings

> **READING CHECK**
>
> Sketches and scenes chosen will vary, but students should choose scenes that are central to the story. These might include the first meeting between Lob and Sandy, one of Lob's returns after escaping from his first owner, the scene of the accident, or Lob at Sandy's hospital bed.

1. Most students will like Lob because he is devoted, friendly, and a good companion and playmate. Some may find his persistence uncanny.

2. As the narrator points out, "Some people choose their dogs, and some dogs choose their people." Lob adopts Sandy and takes care of her rather than the other way around. Lob travels across the country twice to be with her and apparently returns from the dead to visit her and help her recover from her wounds.

3. The description foreshadows the accident in which a truck traveling down the hill at too high a speed injures Sandy and kills Lob.

4. Lob and Sounder are both amazingly loyal, devoted animals, especially to the one person who "owns" them. Lob, an Alsatian, is a playful companion. Sounder, a mongrel mix of redbone hound and bulldog, works as a hunting dog. Sounder lives an extremely long life, holding onto life in order to see the father one more time. Lob comes back from the dead to visit Sandy.

5. Students should describe a situation in which a pet shows great devotion to them or to members of their family. If they haven't personally experienced this type of relationship with an animal, they may describe one that they have read about or seen on film or on TV. Students should mention specific details that illustrate the animal's devotion.

The Smartest Human I Ever Met: My Brother's Dog Shep / Moco Limping
Making Meanings

READING CHECK

a. Moco has a club foot and hobbles feebly. The speaker would like a dog that is healthy, strong, beautiful, and noble.

b. Shep's owner, the narrator's brother Joseph, is dying.

c. Shep has run off to intercept Joseph's soul. He has left his body in the hills and traveled with Joseph's soul.

---

1. In the case of Moco, some students probably would feel much like the speaker of the poem—wishing that Moco were healthy and strong but loving him anyway. In the case of Shep, students probably would appreciate the dog's loyalty but would not want to see him die.

2. The speaker is badly disappointed because Moco is so different from the dog he really wants. At the same time, he recognizes some selfish pride ("vain heart") in wanting a "better" dog.

3. Sounder, before his injury, is like the dog that the speaker would like to have. He is strong, powerful, and a "brutal hunter." After his injury, Sounder, like Moco, is loyal but hobbled by a bad leg.

4. The narrator has been led to believe that his brother is getting better and doesn't want to believe that his brother is dying. He also cannot understand how Shep would know about it.

5. Shep likes the narrator, hunts with him, and obeys him, but his first loyalty is to Joseph, for whom he will sacrifice anything. Similarly, Sounder loves and obeys the boy, but the dog's first loyalty is to the father, for whom he will sacrifice anything.

Spirits of the Railway: Making Meanings

READING CHECK

a. A flooding river destroys the family farm, and there is no work in the city. Chu has to leave China in order to find work and earn money to support his family.

b. While he is helping to dig a railway tunnel, a dynamite blast explodes early and buries him under a pile of rock.

c. He must bind together chopsticks and straw matting, which will represent the bodies of his father and the other workers. Then, he must carry the bundles to the top of the mountain, cover them with soil, and pour tea over them.

---

1. Answers will vary widely, but might include the younger Chu's climb to the mountain top or the appearance of the older Chu's ghost. Explanations will vary.

2. Students may describe the son as courageous, hard-working, reliable, or respectful.

3. Both the older Chu and the father in *Sounder* must take great risks to provide for their families. Both are isolated from their families as a result. Although not a convict, Chu works under dangerous conditions on a work gang and is killed in a dynamite blast. The father toils on a labor gang and is severely injured in a dynamite blast. Both are able to appear to their sons after they have suffered terrible accidents.

4. The Chinese workers suffer from cruel prejudice. They are paid more poorly than their white counterparts, assigned dangerous tasks without necessary warnings, and treated poorly by their white bosses. In death, they are denied proper burial.

5. Students may respond that both fathers would be justified in viewing their labor as unjustly harsh, and their fatal injuries as the result of cruel working conditions.

Learning to Read and Write
Making Meanings

> **READING CHECK**
>
> The wife of Douglass's master teaches him his ABCs. He then gets white boys in the neighborhood to give him lessons. He practices reading a book called *The Columbian Orator.* He copies the letters written by ship's carpenters on pieces of timber. Douglass tricks neighborhood boys into teaching him to write other letters. He copies the letters from a spelling book, and he writes in the blank spaces of Master Thomas's copybook, copying his writing.

1. Students' answers should reflect an awareness of the injustices, anger, frustrations, and discontent that Douglass felt.

2. Reading brought him into contact with published ideas about human rights. He learned the arguments against slavery and became more aware of his own wretched condition and the seeming hopelessness of his situation.

3. Perhaps because slavery placed her in a position of power over another human being, she was inspired to exercise her power to control Douglass. She feared the consequences of having an educated slave around her because of warnings from her husband.

4. Most students will acknowledge that although Douglass was made unhappy as a result of what he learned, he ultimately was better off because of his education. They should recognize that although education made Douglass unhappy as a young man, Douglass the narrator clearly realizes the value of education.

5. Students may suggest that both want a formal education, and that each has to overcome major obstacles to gain knowledge. Whereas Douglass is prohibited by his owner from learning to read, the boy is prevented by his circumstances from learning. Both of them face very limited futures without an education.

6. Answers will be personal and need not be shared, but most students will identify with Douglass's feelings of frustration, anger, and injustice.

Lonesome Valley / I Believe I Can Fly
Making Meanings

> **READING CHECK**
>
> a. Answers may be similar to the following: Life is a lonely journey that each person must take by himself or herself.
>
> b. Answers may be similar to the following: People can do anything if they just believe in their goals and in themselves.

1. Answers will vary. Students should recognize the optimism expressed in "I Believe I Can Fly" and the attitude of endurance and long-suffering expressed in "Lonesome Valley."

2. The lyrics to both versions are informal English that include some colloquialisms, such as *ain't.* The version in *Sounder,* however, is even more informal, including words like *gotta* and *gonna.* This form of English suggests the dialect that the mother speaks, which might account for Armstrong's choice.

3. Students should recognize that the boy in *Sounder* would agree with the message in the song. He believes in his dream of an education and pursues it steadily. Likewise, he believes that he will find his father, and continues his search for years.

4. Students probably will choose "I Believe I Can Fly"—not only because it is contemporary but also because it corresponds closely with the goals of education, which include preparing students to "fly"—to believe in themselves and in their potential to achieve any of their goals. Some students, however, may find the stoic pessimism of "Lonesome Valley" more compelling.

David and Goliath: Making Meanings

READING CHECK

a. If the champion of the army of Israel kills Goliath, then the Philistines will become servants of the people of Israel. If Goliath defeats the champion of the army of Israel, then the army of Israel will become servants of the Philistines.

b. He believes that the Lord is on the side of Israel and has felt the Lord's help in the past.

c. David fires a stone from his sling at Goliath. The stone hits Goliath in the forehead and kills him.

---

1. Answers may resemble the following:

   - If I were standing before Goliath, I would be terrified because he is so huge and powerful.

   - If I were in the Philistine army and saw Goliath killed, I would wonder how such a modest opponent could defeat our enormous champion.

2. The reader is impressed by the size and quality of Goliath's arms and armor—and by the strength and size of Goliath, who must wear and use this equipment.

3. He may be convinced by David's argument that the Lord will give him victory over Goliath.

4. The boy sees the guard as an evil giant, like Goliath, who seems too powerful to be defeated. The Bible story might reassure him that even a young boy is not helpless, for the Lord can protect him against the mightiest giant. His anger might also lead him to enjoy the thought of the guard's downfall.

5. Some students may believe that this is good advice, for people need to believe in the possibility of winning against great odds. Other students may say that confronting enormous odds on a daily basis can lead to constant defeat and frustration.

Reading Skills and Strategies Worksheets

Chapters I–II: Visualizing Scenes

Details in the scenes and captions will vary, and students need not have special artistic talent to capture the details that they consider important. The following are possible captions:

The Boy Takes Pride in Sounder: "There ain't no dog like Sounder," the boy says.

A Delicious, Dangerous Smell: On a winter's morning, the boy is surprised to find what's on the stove.

The Sheriff Arrives: The sheriff and his deputies are cruel and prejudiced.

Sounder to the Rescue: Although the boy tries to hold him back, Sounder breaks free and runs after the wagon to which his master has been chained.

Chapters III–V: Charting Causes and Effects

Answers will vary. A sample answer is provided below.

CAUSE	EFFECT
The mother knows that her son will crawl under the cabin, looking for Sounder.	She makes him put on old clothes for protection.
The boy is desperate to find Sounder, whether the dog is alive or dead.	The boy disobeys his mother and leaves the younger children alone at home.
The boy's mother plans to bake two Christmas cakes.	The boy's mother brings home vanilla flavoring.
Women are not allowed to visit the jail in town.	The boy takes the cake to his father.
The man at the jail thinks that a tool could be hidden in the cake.	The man at the jail breaks the cake into pieces.
Sounder finally has returned home.	The boy hears whining on the cabin porch.

Chapters VI–VIII: Using a Time Line

Answers will vary. A possible sequence of events follows.

1. The boy goes in search of his father.

2. Outside a road camp, the boy has his fingers smashed by a piece of iron thrown by a guard.

3. The boy finds a book in a trash barrel and tries to understand the stories.

4. A teacher tends to the boy's injury and invites him to come to school.

5. The mother urges her son to go away to school.

6. A few years later, the father returns, disabled from an accident in the prison quarry.

7. The father dies.

8. Sounder dies.

Literary Elements Worksheets

Imagery

Answers will vary. A sample answer is provided below.

1. The passage appeals to the reader's senses of sight, touch, hearing, and possibly smell. "Sight" words and phrases include *walnuts to fall, brownish-green husks, oozing their dark purple stain, flat rock,* and possibly *first hard frost.*

2. The passage appeals primarily to the reader's senses of sight and touch. "Touch" words and phrases include *warm stovepipe, glowing warmth,* and *warmth ran up his sleeves and down over his ribs inside his shirt and soaked inward.*

3. The passage appeals to the reader's senses of sight, touch, taste, smell, and possibly hearing. "Taste" words and phrases include *dry dust* and *tasted like lime and grease.*

4. The passage appeals to the reader's senses of sight, touch, and hearing. "Hearing" words and phrases include *the rocker began to squeak, began to rock,* and *picked out walnut kernels.*

5. Images will vary. Encourage students to be specific in their explanations.

Answer Key (continued)

Allusion

2. The boy fears for his father's safety in jail, wonders what will happen to him there, and hopes that his father will be rescued soon.

3. The boy is about to go on a journey in search of his father, but wants to remind his mother that there is hope for a successful outcome.

4. The family can overcome hardship. Despite hard times, their dreams can turn out even better than they had imagined.

5. The boy does not need to be afraid during his lonely search, for he can be sure he will win.

6. The boy sees the cruel guard as a great enemy and would like to see the guard brought down.

Vocabulary Worksheet

If you wish to score this worksheet, assign the point values given in parentheses.

A. *(5 points each)*

1. punctuated	6. sanctuary
2. mongrel	7. cistern
3. haunches	8. tote
4. mange	9. fruitless
5. sultry	10. parched

B. *(5 points each)*

11. b	16. d
12. c	17. a
13. a	18. c
14. b	19. d
15. a	20. a

Test

Part I: Objective Questions

1. T	5. F	9. T	13. a
2. F	6. T	10. F	14. b
3. F	7. F	11. c	15. c
4. T	8. T	12. d	

Part II: Short-Answer Questions

16. The dog has a powerful, melodic voice with a sound that carries across the valley when he is hunting.

17. It is windy, and the raccoons and possums don't move around much in the wind. The raccoons may have left the area.

18. There is a tear on his overalls, and the cloth matches a scrap found at the smokehouse.

19. The deputy shoots him when he runs to protect the father, who is being taken away.

20. She returns the food to its owners.

21. He tells the boy he doesn't want him to visit him again.

22. He is carrying the book he found in the trash can.

23. The teacher has two stoves, two lamps burning at once, and books everywhere.

24. The dog races down the road to meet the father and barks for the first time since the man was taken away.

25. He is injured in a dynamite explosion while working in a quarry.

Answer Key (continued)

Part III: Essay Questions

Students should respond to two out of the five essay topics. Answers will vary but should include specific references to the text.

a. The novel takes place somewhere in the south-eastern United States around a hundred years ago. Students should recognize that setting is crucial to the plot of *Sounder* in at least two ways. For example, the time of the novel is important because during that period in history, African Americans frequently were the victims of an unjust legal system, were disproportionately sentenced to labor on work gangs, and rarely had access to a formal education. There were no telephones, so it would have been difficult for the family to keep in touch with the father. The family lives in an isolated sharecropper's cabin, limiting opportunities to get an education and making them more dependent upon their own resources, such as hunting.

b. Many students will conclude that the novel is optimistic because the boy has succeeded in getting an education and thus has a brighter future than seemed likely at the beginning of the novel. Other students will conclude that the novel is pessimistic because both the father and Sounder are injured and later die.

c. Students should recognize that by not giving the characters names, Armstrong has attempted to make them universal. If they were given names, the reader would see them more clearly as individuals. The reader might have more sympathy for named characters but perhaps would not appreciate their greater symbolic meaning.

d. Students may describe several different ways in which religion plays a role in the novel. These may include the spirituals the mother hums and sings, the Bible stories the boy thinks of while he travels, the characters from the Bible the mother talks about when times are hard, the spiritual comfort the mother finds at the time of her husband's death, and the scripture read aloud at the father's burial.

e. Students probably will address a theme that relates to love, racial injustice, the pursuit of knowledge, or persistence in reaching goals. They should demonstrate an awareness of the importance of the theme in the novel and give examples of how it is developed. For example, love is displayed between family members. The boy travels the state looking for his father. His father steals and then survives imprisonment, hard labor, and terrible injury out of love for his family. Sounder is injured out of love for his master and lives a long life waiting for his master's return. Racial injustice is seen in the treatment of the father by the sheriff, the treatment of the boy by the white prison guard, and more subtly in the social conditions that condemn the family to poverty, limited opportunities, and a lack of education. The pursuit of knowledge is demonstrated by the boy's love for the stories his mother tells, by his desire to have a book, by his effort to learn to read store signs and newspapers, in his joy at finding a book, and in his decision to stay with the teacher and learn. Persistence in goals is seen in the boy's search for Sounder and in his search for his father, which, though unsuccessful, demonstrates his inner drive.